I0202059

SPIRITUAL MINISTRY

1990 North East Christian Conference
@ Harvey Cedars NJ

Stephen Kaung

Copyright © 2015
Christian Testimony Ministry
Richmond, Virginia
All Rights Reserved

ISBN: 978-1-942521-67-9

Available from:

Christian Testimony Ministry
4424 Huguenot Road
Richmond, Virginia 23235

www.christiantestimonyministry.com

Printed in USA

CONTENTS

The spoken words have been transcribed by permission with only minimal editing for clarity. Unless otherwise indicated, Scripture quotations are from the New Translation by J. N. Darby.

MINISTRY TO THE LORD

Ezekiel 44:15-31—But the priests, the Levites, the sons of Zadok, that kept the charge of my sanctuary when the children of Israel went astray from me, they shall approach unto me to minister unto me, and they shall stand before me to present unto me the fat and the blood, saith the Lord Jehovah. They shall enter into my sanctuary, and they shall approach unto my table, to minister unto me, and they shall keep my charge. And it shall come to pass when they enter in at the gates of the inner court, they shall be clothed with linen garments; and no wool shall come upon them, when they minister in the gates of the inner court, and towards the house. They shall have linen tires upon their heads, and shall have linen breeches upon their loins; they shall not gird on anything that causeth sweat. And when they go forth into the outer court, into the outer court to the people, they shall put off their garments wherein they ministered, and lay them in the holy cells; and they shall put on other garments, that they may not hallow the people with their garments. Neither shall they shave their heads, nor suffer their locks to grow long: they shall duly poll their heads. Neither shall any priest drink wine when they enter into the inner court. And they shall not take for their wives a widow, nor her that is put away; but they shall take maidens of the seed of the house of Israel, or a widow that is the widow of a priest. And they shall teach my people the difference between holy and profane, and cause them to discern between unclean and clean. And in controversy they shall stand to judge: they shall judge it according to my judgments; and they shall keep my laws and my statutes in all my solemnities; and they shall hallow my sabbaths. And they shall come at no dead person to become unclean; but for father, or for mother, or for son, or for daughter, for brother, or for sister that hath had no husband, they may become unclean. And after he is cleansed, they shall count unto him seven days. And on the day that he goeth into the sanctuary, unto the inner court, to minister in the sanctuary, he shall present his sin- offering, saith the Lord Jehovah. And it shall be unto them for an inheritance; I am their inheritance: and ye shall give them no possession in Israel; I am their possession. They shall eat the oblation and the sin-

offering and the trespass- offering; and every devoted thing in Israel shall be theirs. And the first of all the first-fruits of every kind, and every heave-offering of every kind, of all your heave-offerings, shall be for the priests; ye shall also give unto the priest the first of your dough, that he may cause the blessing to rest on thy house. The priests shall not eat of anything that dieth of itself, or of that which is torn, whether of fowl or of beast.

Acts 13:1-3—Now there were in Antioch, in the assembly which was there, prophets and teachers: Barnabas, and Simeon who was called Niger, and Lucius the Cyrenian, and Manaen, foster-brother of Herod the tetrach, and Saul. And as they were ministering to the Lord and fasting, the Holy Spirit said, Separate me now Barnabas and Saul for the work to which I have called them. Then, having fasted and prayed, and having laid their hands on them, they let them go.

Shall we pray:

Dear heavenly Father, as we gather here in Thy presence, we realize that we are standing on holy ground. By Thy grace, we remove our shoes. We stand humbly before Thee as Thy bondslaves of love; and we do ask Thee, Lord, that Thou will speak to us through Thy Word. Lord, Thou knowest our condition, Thou knowest our hearts; Thou knowest how we do desire that we may be a people that will really please Thee, that will really satisfy Thee, that will really do Thy will. Oh our Father, we just come presenting ourselves afresh to Thee, asking that Thou will speak to each of us in such a way that we may be completely delivered from what we are now to what Thou want us to be. We do commit this time into Thy hands, knowing that unless Thy Holy Spirit brings Thy Word into our hearts, we will not be able to see or hear or be lifted up unto Thyself. So we just look to Thee for this time. Oh, how we praise and thank Thee because Thou art merciful, Thou art gracious, and Thou art ever ready to bring us to Thy will. We ask in the name of our Lord Jesus. Amen.

Our burden for this time together is this matter of spiritual ministry. Now when we mention the word *ministry*, probably, the first thought that comes to our mind is prophetic ministry or the ministry of the Word. We remember that the apostle said, "We will give ourselves to prayer and the ministry of the

Word." But prophetic ministry or ministry of the Word is not given to all believers. Even though all believers may prophesy in the sense that we find in I Corinthians 14—we may all be used of God to exhort one another, to encourage one another, and to comfort one another—to have a prophetic ministry or to be called to the ministry of the Word is something that is given to some but not to all. So this is not what we are sharing at this time.

Again, when we mention the word *ministry*, probably, what immediately comes to your mind is this matter of so-called ministry —entering into the ministry, being ordained into the ministry. But this is not what we are talking about. The spiritual ministry we are talking about is a ministry that every believer, everyone redeemed of the Lord is called into. Therefore, the first thing I would like to emphasize is that every child of God, everyone redeemed of the Lord, all of us are called into a spiritual ministry. None of us who are redeemed of the Lord is an exception; everyone is called into a spiritual ministry. After we have settled this, then we can go on and talk about this whole matter of spiritual ministry in which we are all involved.

Actually, there are two parts in this spiritual ministry. One is ministry unto the Lord, and the other is ministry unto the house of the Lord. Or to put it another way, in this ministry in which we all are involved, there is priestly ministry, which is mainly unto the Lord; and then there is Levitical ministry, the ministry of the Levites, and it is mainly unto the people or the house of God. It is a very unfortunate thing that, today, God's people are more familiar with ministry unto the house of God than with ministry unto the Lord. Lots of ministries that we are involved with are in this area of ministry unto the house of God or unto the people of God. That occupies most of our so-called spiritual ministry. We know very little of and we are involved very little in this matter of ministry unto the Lord. Probably, we do not even know what ministry unto the Lord is, and yet, it is the foundation of all ministries. Unless we minister unto the Lord, we cannot minister unto the Lord's people. Unless we know how to minister unto the Lord, our ministry unto the house of God will be superficial, will be shallow, will be temporary. There will not be that eternal and spiritual value in it. This is a great need among God's people today. So we would like to focus our attention on this matter of ministry unto the Lord.

THE FIRST PRINCIPLE OF SPIRITUAL MINISTRY

When God called the children of Israel out of Egypt, His purpose for this redeemed people was for them to become a nation of priests; and as priests, their primary occupation was to minister unto the Lord. That was what God was really after in His people. But unfortunately, the children of Israel sinned and forfeited this honor, this privilege of ministering unto the Lord, and eventually, this whole people were disqualified.

God chose the tribe of Levites from among the twelve to serve the house, and of that tribe of Levites, God chose the family of Aaron to be priests. In the Old Testament, we find that the priests were to offer sacrifices unto the Lord, light the lamps in the holy place, place the shewbread on the table, and burn incense at the golden altar of incense. They were the people who drew near to God and ministered unto Him. The Levites

11

were to keep the doors of the tabernacle lest strangers came in. They were to serve in the tabernacle—bringing the water, bringing the wood, and doing all the things under the direction of the priests. Their job was to serve the house, the tabernacle, the people of God. When any child of Israel came to offer a sacrifice, they would help him slay the animal; that was their work. The rest of the children of Israel, in a sense, were completely barred from service, both to the house and to the Lord. And we know that it was a great failure.

In the New Testament, we find that God does not want us to go back to the system that was God's emergency measure, not His original design. In the New Testament, through His redemption, our Lord Jesus is bringing us back to God's original purpose. That is the reason, after we are saved, He makes us a kingdom of priests. We are all to serve as priests before God. Our purpose on this earth is one: *We are to minister unto the Lord.*

Probably, we need to ask ourselves this question: Do we really live our life on earth ministering unto the Lord? How do we minister unto the Lord? One day, when I was reading the book of Acts, I came to Acts 13 where you find five prophets and teachers in the church in Antioch. First in the list is Barnabas. We know Barnabas. If you go back to Acts 4, you find his former name was Joseph. He was a Levite, but he loved the Lord. He laid everything at the feet of the Lord; and the apostles gave him the name: Barnabas, son of consolation. Barnabas was a man full of the Holy Spirit. He was sent to Antioch to see what the Lord was doing there, and when he saw what the Lord was doing, his heart was so warmed. He stayed with them, exhorting them and encouraging them. That was Barnabas.

Then there was Simeon who was called Niger. In other words, he must have been a brother who came from Africa. There was Lucius, the Cyrenian, and Manaen who was the foster-brother of Herod the tetrach; he came from a noble family. Last in the list was Saul, that great Pharisee who met the Lord on the road to Damascus. The Lord put these five brothers together, and they were prophets and teachers.

What is the function of prophets and teachers? The function of the prophets and teachers is to speak to the people of God. They minister to the people of God. They minister the Word of God to God's people; but here you find these five prophets and teachers were ministering unto the Lord. They should have been ministering unto the people, but here they were ministering unto the Lord. They were not actively engaged in speaking, in prophesying, in teaching. Instead, they were ministering unto the Lord.

This matter of ministering unto the Lord arrested my heart. I began to ask the Lord what it meant. Why was it that these five, who were supposed to be busily engaged in teaching the people, in presenting the will, the mind of God to the people to build them up—which was their work—seemed to be inactive? They were not doing their job. They had set themselves apart to minister unto the Lord. What were they doing there? It dawned upon me that these brothers knew that unless they first ministered unto the Lord, they could not minister unto the people of God. How unfortunate that we often think we can minister to the people of God. If God gives us the gift to prophesy, if God gives us the gift to teach, surely we can do the job. But we fail to realize that even though God may call you and gift you, yet if you do not know the first principle of spiritual ministry, your ministry unto the house of God will be ineffective. We need to minister unto the Lord first, and only afterwards are we able to minister unto the house of God.

I wondered what they did when they ministered unto the Lord. Then I was directed to Ezekiel 44 because there it tells us how to minister unto the Lord.

JUDGMENT AND RESTORATION OF SPIRITUAL MINISTRY

We know that Ezekiel was a prophet in exile. The children of Israel had rebelled against God and they were taken into Babylonian captivity. Ezekiel was among those captives, but God called him to be a prophet. The last nine chapters of the book of Ezekiel, from chapters 40-48, are the visions that God gave to Ezekiel of the final restoration of all things. God is going to restore all things. He will restore the temple. The temple in Jerusalem was destroyed completely, but one day, He will restore that temple. It is not the temple that the remnant, after seventy years of captivity, returned and built, but the final temple; it is not the physical one but the spiritual one. And God gave Ezekiel a vision of that temple.

God also desires to restore the priesthood, the service in the temple, the kingship, the kingdom, the city. So you find these nine chapters of the book of Ezekiel are a prophecy of the final restoration. Everything will be restored to God's original purpose. That is the vision that was given to the prophet Ezekiel. And in this vision, there is a part, in chapter 44, that speaks of the restoration of spiritual ministry.

Before that spiritual ministry was restored, you find, first of all, there was God's judgment on spiritual ministry. When the children of Israel forsook God and began to worship idols, unfortunately, the Levites were also led astray. They even helped the people to worship idols. Not only the Levites but even the priests began to serve at the altars of the idols. This whole matter was such an abomination in the sight of God. So even when God is to restore spiritual ministry,

His judgment is still there. When the children of Israel went astray, the Levites helped them in their rebellion against God; therefore, the iniquity was upon them. God forgave them but, because of this, they were not able to enter into the sanctuary and minister unto the Lord Himself. God still allowed them to keep the doors of the future temple, to serve in the temple, and to minister to the people, but they were not allowed to minister unto the Lord Himself; only the sons of Zadok could do that. The reason why the priests were mentioned is because it showed that not only the Levites were not restored to God's original design of ministry unto the Lord but even the priests were not restored. Among the priests, only the sons of Zadok were called by God to minister unto Himself. Why? It was because during the declension, when the children of Israel fell away from the Lord and the Levites and probably most of the priests fell away, the sons of Zadok were faithful to the Lord. They kept the charge of God. Because of their faithfulness, God said, "In the restoration, they are the ones permitted to draw near to Me to minister unto Me."

THE FAITHFUL MAY MINISTER TO THE LORD

Here you find a spiritual principle: *All who are forgiven can minister to the house, but only those who are faithful may minister unto the Lord.* To minister unto the Lord is not a small thing. In the vision of Ezekiel, the glory of the Lord entered into the house, the temple. The Lord was there, and for people to draw near to Him to minister unto Him was an awesome thing. God is holy, God is righteous, God is full of glory; and to be able to come near to Him and really minister unto Him, as if ministering to His needs, to satisfy His heart—that is a tremendous honor. It is not something that can be thrown to anybody. Do not think that ministering unto the Lord is a small thing. It is a tremendous honor. As those who are forgiven, we all can minister to the house of God, but only the faithful can minister unto the Lord.

In a sense, the church is still in captivity. The church is in captivity to the world, not only to the world as it is but also to the religious world. As you read church history, even though from generation to generation there were some who, by the grace and mercy of God, were brought back to Jerusalem to be at peace with God and were built up as a kind of token or emblem of the house of God that God is after, as a whole, even to our day, we have to acknowledge that the church is still in captivity.

When the people of God fall away, who are those that will be faithful to the Lord and keep the charge of God? In other words, when you find there is declension everywhere, who are those people who will be faithful to the original purpose of God, faithful to the testimony of the Lord Jesus? And to those who are faithful, this privilege of ministry unto the Lord Himself will be given.

In the letters that Paul wrote to Timothy, he mentioned time and again, especially in II Timothy, this matter of faithfulness: entrust to the faithful. It cannot be entrusted to everybody because people are falling away from God and from His purpose. Therefore, there are some who are still faithful; entrust to them the testimony of Jesus.

Who are the faithful ones? The church has become a great house. In I Timothy, you find the church is the church of the living God, the pillar and base of truth. Yet, when you come to II Timothy, you find that the church has become a big house, a great house; and in that great house, there are vessels of honor and vessels of dishonor, vessels of gold and silver and vessels of wood and earth. The Scripture says if you have purified yourself, separated yourself from the vessels to dishonor, then you will become sanctified, acceptable and ready for the Master's use. In other words, today, God is looking for those who are faithful to His testimony, faithful to His purpose; those who have purified themselves from that which is unfaithful. It is only to those who are faithful that there is the privilege of ministering unto the Lord.

So before we talk about this matter of ministry unto the Lord, we really need to humble ourselves before Him. Thank God, He has forgiven us; but have we been faithful to Him in this time of declension? And if we are faithful, then the Lord says, "You may minister unto Me." I wonder whether that is the reason why we see lots of ministry unto the house but very little, if any, ministry unto the Lord.

DRAWING NEAR TO THE LORD

What is ministry unto the Lord? "But the priests, the Levites, the sons of Zadok, that kept the charge of my sanctuary when the children of Israel went astray from me, they shall approach unto me" (Ezekiel 44:15). To minister unto the Lord, the first thing is to approach, to draw near to the Lord. You cannot minister unto the Lord if you are a thousand miles away from Him. You have to draw near to Him to serve Him. But this approaching Him in Ezekiel 44 is different from the approaching Him in Hebrews 10. Hebrews 10 tells us that, through the blood of our Lord Jesus, a new and living way has been opened for us; the veil was rent, that is, His body was broken for us; and He is our great High Priest interceding for us unceasingly. On the basis of these three things, we may approach the Holy of Holies with boldness; we may come to God with confidence. But for what reason do we approach Him? We approach Him to receive grace to live. If we do not approach Him, we cannot live even a minute. Today, we are still living. Today, by the grace of God, we are still being kept. It is all because of the blood of the Lamb. It is all because of the broken body of our

Lord Jesus. It is all because of His high priesthood. It is all because of what He has done for us that we are able to receive mercy, to receive grace even to live on this earth. Thank God for this approach. But if you read Ezekiel 44, you find when God said, "You shall approach unto Me," it is not in the sense that you may receive grace for your needs but it is to minister unto Him. Now that is a great difference.

We all know and, thank God, we all experience that approach unto the Lord to receive grace and mercy for seasonable help; but do we know this approach, this drawing near to Him? It is not to receive grace to meet our needs, but it is to minister to Him, as it were, to meet His need. Only those who live near to Him can serve Him. Even on earth, for those people who are chosen to be near a king or queen to serve daily, it is a privilege, it is an honor. Everybody cannot do that but only those chosen few who are privileged to be companions with a king and be near him all the time to minister to him. How much more it is for us to minister unto the Lord, to be, as it were, His daily companion, to approach Him at all times and learn to minister to His needs. It requires a life that lives very close to Him.

If we look into our lives, how close are we to the Lord? Is it that we find ourselves, oftentimes, quite distant from Him? The world seems to come upon us and draw us away from the Lord into the world. Maybe in the early morning when you have a time with the Lord, you sense that intimacy with Him; but when you step into the world, it seems as if that closeness, that nearness vanishes. Can we live a life on this earth that is busily engaged with external things and yet within our heart have a closeness, an intimacy, a fellowship with the Lord that is unhindered? We need to live continuously in His presence in spite of the fact that, outwardly, we live among the people of this world. What He desires is our being with Him more than what we do for Him. This is ministry unto the Lord.

I wonder if this is the reason why we find it so easy, or comparatively easier, to minister to God's people, to the house of God, than to minister unto the Lord. Approaching Him, drawing near to Him, living constantly in His presence is something that satisfies His heart.

STANDING BEFORE THE LORD

"They shall stand before Me." Again, this "standing before Him" is different from the judicial standing before Him that we all have. Formerly, we could not stand before Him because we were sinners; and if we were to stand before Him, we would be smitten to death. But thank God, through the redemption of our Lord Jesus, we have a standing before God because we are clothed with Christ. When God looks upon us, He does not see us, He sees Christ; and that is the reason why we are accepted by God in the Beloved. Thank God for this standing that we all have. But the standing here is a deeper thing. It is not just a matter of us standing there and not being smitten; it is standing before the Lord in order that we may minister unto Him.

When you read the Old Testament, there is one phrase that will catch your heart, and that is what Elijah said: "I am the one who stands before God" (see I Kings 17:1, 18:15). He was a person who stood before God. Before he stood before

Ahab, he stood before God; and even when he stood before Ahab, he was still a person who stood before God. It was not just an occasional thing, but it had become almost like a status. That is what he was—a man who stood before God. Do you know what standing before God is? Do you know that standing, from the eyes of the flesh, is inactive, is passive? Our flesh cannot stand standing. We are on the move all the time; that is our flesh. We think that only as we are running hither and thither, doing this thing and that thing and being actively involved, then it is worthwhile. If we are doing nothing—not even walking—but standing, that is a waste of time. The flesh cannot stand standing. Try it. Try to stand before the Lord. Of course, this does not mean physically standing; it means an attitude. You need to develop an attitude to minister unto the Lord. You need to become a person who is always standing before the Lord.

In the Word of God, standing before the Lord is such an honor. In the vision that Zechariah saw of the lampstand and the two olive trees by the side of the lampstand, an explanation was given that these were the two sons of oil who stood before the Lord.

Unto thee do I lift up mine eyes, O thou that dwellest in the heavens. Behold, as the eyes of servants look unto the hand of their masters, as the eyes of a maiden unto the hand of her mistress, so our eyes are directed to Jehovah our God, until he be gracious unto us. (Psalm 123:1-2)

That is standing. This Psalm was written with a background. In the Orient, in the East, when a master entertains guests, his servants stand around the room with their eyes upon the master. It is not considered a good thing for the master to open his mouth and tell his servants what to do. So the custom is that the servants will be standing there, alert and waiting. They are not standing there dreaming or sleeping but they are watchful, with their eyes upon the hands of the master. The master will not say a word. When anything needs to be done, he just uses his hand to make a gesture, and the servants know exactly what to do and will go ahead and do it. Now that is standing before the Lord.

Brothers and sisters, are we running around? Are we so impatient we cannot wait upon the Lord? So-called ministry, today, is just people running around doing things according to what they think is good or according to what they think is the will of God. As a matter of fact, lots of so-called Christian activities today do not originate from the Master. It is working for God, not working with God. Unless we know how to stand before Him, unless we know how to wait upon Him until we receive orders, there is no movement. People will say: "You are lazy. You are idling." You will be criticized and you will be misunderstood. But only those who know God would rather stand before Him and do nothing than do anything before the order is given. Are you sure that what you are doing is the will of God? Are you certain that God has commanded you to run? The sin of presumption is the same as the sin of disobedience. If God gives you an order and you do not do it, it is the sin of disobedience. But if the Lord has not given you orders and you go ahead, it is the sin of presumption. No wonder the Psalmist prayed, "Deliver me from presumptuous sins" (see Psalm 19:13). Today, God's people know very little of the sin of presumption.

Probably, we know to disobey God is sin; we realize that. But do we realize that doing something without His order is also sin? If we can be kept from the sin of presumption, then we will be perfect before Him. That is what the Psalmist said in Psalm 19:13.

To wait upon Him, to stand before Him is to pray. You are praying to know His will, praying for His kingdom to come, praying for His will to be done on earth as it is in heaven. Again, I say it is not easy for the flesh. We cannot do it. It is only by the mercies of God that we are able to stand before Him that we may minister unto Him. This very attitude of standing is a ministry unto the Lord.

PRESENTING THE FAT AND THE BLOOD TO THE LORD

"They shall stand before me to present unto me the fat and the blood, saith the Lord Jehovah." To understand this, you have to go back to Leviticus which is the handbook of the priests. In Leviticus 3, you will find that when the children offered peace offerings before God, the blood and all the fat of the sacrifice was offered. It is described in detail. The net, the kidney and all those fats of the animal were to be burned on the altar as an offering of sweet savor. In the same chapter, you find that the fat is the food of the offering; it is for God to consume. None of the children of Israel could eat the fat or drink the blood because they were devoted to the Lord. So here you find what those who minister unto the Lord do. They are privileged to present unto the Lord the fat and the blood.

The Fat

What is the fat? What does it signify? Today, we do not like fat; but in the Scriptures, fat is a beautiful thing. Where does fat come from? You need fuel for your life, so when you eat, you put fuel into your body and you are able to live. But if you have extra, an abundance, then it is preserved as fat in your body. As a matter of fact, fat signifies the abundance, the excellence, the vitality, the energy of life. And the fat of the sacrifice was to be consumed by the Lord Himself as His food.

Primarily, of course, the sacrifice speaks of Christ. When you think of our Lord Jesus, you find such beauty in His life, such energy; you find such abundant life in Him; and His whole life was offered on the altar as food to God. No wonder God said, "This is My beloved Son in whom I have found My delight." In union with Christ, with His life in us, when we experience life abundant—that vitality, that power, that beauty, that strength—it is not for us to consume, nor is it to be consumed by anybody else. It is to be completely offered to God to be His food.

Remember, it is not your fat or my fat. It is not our natural energy, natural life, natural strength. Oh, how we have abundance of natural strength! How we have abundance of natural mind! How we have abundance of natural this and natural that! And we want to offer all these on the altar. No; these are abominable to God. He does not want them. "Present your bodies a living sacrifice" (Romans 12:1). So, I present my body a living sacrifice. But remember, that body is not the body of death nor the body of sin; it is the body redeemed by the Lord. If you want to offer your original body, that is, your natural body and all the natural strength in your body, that is your natural fat; and it is no good. It is only that which is of Him that is constituted in us that is acceptable to the Lord.

Most of us, in a sense, are able to draw from the Lord just barely enough to live on. There is no abundance, and without that abundance, how can we minister unto the Lord? But those who are in union with Him, those who know His life abundant, those who have that spiritual reserve are privileged to present spiritual sacrifices acceptable to God through Jesus Christ. That is the offering of the fat.

The Blood

There is the presenting of the blood, not only in the sense that when you believe in the Lord Jesus, His blood atones your sins; but the closer you live to the Lord, the more you find the preciousness of the blood. Without the blood, you cannot live a moment. If we walk in the light as He is in the light, we have fellowship one with another, and the blood of God's Son, Jesus Christ, cleanses us from all our sins. We need to present the blood to God continuously.

Brother Watchman Nee said, "The blood is to satisfy God's holiness and righteousness, and the fat is to satisfy God's glory." Are we presenting the blood before the Lord to satisfy God's holiness and righteousness all the time? When He sees the blood, His holiness and righteousness are satisfied. Are we presenting the fat continuously to Him? When He sees His beloved Son, His glory is satisfied. This is our daily life. Our daily life is a continuous presenting of the fat and of the blood of the Lord Jesus that we have experienced, that we have appreciated and known.

APPROACHING THE TABLE

"They shall approach unto my table." Now if the table speaks of the table of shewbread, then we know that it is in the holy place. Only the priests can enter into the holy place and put the shewbread on that table. The shewbread literally means the bread of the presence. In other words, this shewbread is a type of our Lord Jesus. He is the bread of the presence, and He is ever present before the Father. That is the Father's joy and delight. After a week, this bread was taken away and changed for the new bread, and the bread was to be the food for the priests (see Leviticus 24:5-9). So those who minister unto the Lord present Christ to God to be His satisfaction. At the same time, they are in communion with Christ and are satisfied and filled with Him. So it speaks of communion. We commune with the Lord; and in communing, we are putting the shewbread on the table.

Naturally speaking, no joy can be compared to the joy of a father seeing the son, especially if the son is very loyal and very obedient. How much more our heavenly Father is pleased when we present Christ to Him as the shewbread. He sees Christ continuously in us, and we are in constant communion with the Lord. That is ministry unto the Lord.

Some people say that maybe the table does not speak of the table of shewbread because, if you read Ezekiel 41, it seems that the table is the altar of incense. Now if it speaks of the altar of incense, it means worship and praise. That is our privilege.

KEEPING THE TESTIMONY OF THE LORD

"They shall keep my charge." A charge is a command, a burden, or an office. That is the way it is used in Scripture. When the Lord said, "They shall keep my charge," it means that they shall keep His testimony. He will commit Himself to them, and they will keep His testimony faithfully in this world.

CONDITIONS FOR MINISTERING TO THE LORD

No Sweating

When we minister unto the Lord, there are certain conditions that must be fulfilled. All who minister to the Lord have to be clothed with linen garments from the head to the feet. They have the linen tire on their head; they have linen breeches; all the garments are linen. No wool should be upon their body. The reason given is that when you minister unto the Lord, there can be no sweating.

In the outer court, there is lots of sweating. When you drag a sheep or a bullock, there is sweating. When you draw this bullock to the altar, tie it to the horns of the altar and slaughter it,

34

there is sweating. In the outer court there is lots of sweating; but when you enter into the sanctuary, when you come to minister unto the Lord Himself, no sweating is allowed.

What is sweat? It comes out from the body; it is our natural strength. Anything that comes from our natural strength is sweating. And how much of God's work today is a work of sweating! You have to plan and plot; you have to sell; you have to advertise; you have to convince; you have to attract; you have to negotiate; you have to do all kinds of things in order to make a work *work*. That is sweating.

But when you come to minister unto the Lord, no natural strength, nothing that comes out of you is allowed. Now if you put woolen garments upon you, surely you will sweat. As a matter of fact, there is no window in the holy place. It is all closed in, and of course, the air is probably a little bit warm. So you will sweat if you wear a woolen garment. Everything has to be linen; and linen, in the Scriptures, always speaks of the life of our Lord Jesus. His whole life upon this earth was like a linen garment. His righteousness is bright and shiny. We need to be clothed completely with Christ. As we minister unto the Lord, we minister to Him out of Christ, not out of ourselves. That is the reason everything has to be in linen.

No Extremes

When you minister unto the Lord, you cannot shave your head nor can you allow your hair to grow long, but you must poll your head. When you shave your head, it is a sign of rebellion. When you let your hair grow long, it is a sign of carelessness. In other words, when you come to minister unto the Lord, you cannot go to extremes. You cannot be either rebellious or passively careless. You have to be disciplined.

No Influence of the World

When the priests ministered unto the Lord, they could not drink any wine. You have to be sober. You cannot be influenced by the world. You cannot bring anything of the world into ministry to the Lord.

Nothing of the Flesh

You cannot touch any dead body because that will make you defiled and unclean. Dead body, in the Scriptures, always speaks of our flesh. It defiles. There can be nothing of the flesh, not even a touch of it.

Kept Pure

You cannot marry any divorced person. You can only marry a maiden or the widow of a priest. That means you have to be kept pure before the Lord. So there are a number of conditions as we come to minister unto the Lord.

Ministering unto the Lord is an awesome thing. Unless we are clean, unless we are pure, unless we are clothed with Christ, unless we are disciplined, how can we come into His presence and stand there beholding His glory? How can we minister unto Him? But thank God, as we minister unto Him, He is our reward. He said: "I am your inheritance. I am your possession. You shall not have any other possession, but I am your possession." Isn't that much better than anything else?

Brothers and sisters, this is ministry unto the Lord. Ministry unto the Lord is something so different from our natural concept. Our natural concept of ministry is work, activities. But when you think of ministry unto the Lord, you find that it is life; it is your standing before Him; it is your waiting upon Him; it is your keeping His charge, being faithful to His testimony. When the world is falling apart, there are people who are faithful to Him. That satisfies His heart. That is ministry unto the Lord. May the Lord help us really to enter into this realm of ministry unto Him.

Shall we pray:

Dear heavenly Father, we do acknowledge that we know very little of this ministry unto Thee. Lord, we ask Thy forgiveness. We pray for light, for understanding, for revelation to deliver us out of what we call ministry and really get us down to that one ministry that is so fundamental, that is the only one that really satisfies, that ministry unto Thee. Help us, Lord, direct us by Thy Spirit that we may be a people who really minister unto Thee. In the name of our Lord Jesus. Amen.

MINISTRY TO THE HOUSE

Ezekiel 44:9-14—Thus saith the Lord Jehovah: No stranger, uncircumcised in heart and uncircumcised in flesh, shall enter into my sanctuary, of any stranger that is among the children of Israel. But the Levites who went away far from me, when Israel went astray, going astray from me after their idols, they shall even bear their iniquity; but they shall be ministers in my sanctuary, having oversight at the gates of the house, and doing the service of the house: they shall slaughter the burnt-offering and the sacrifice for the people, and they shall stand before them to minister unto them. Because they ministered unto them before their idols, and were unto the house of Israel a stumbling-block of iniquity; therefore have I lifted up my hand against them, saith the Lord Jehovah, that they shall bear their iniquity. And they shall not draw near unto me, to do the [service] of a priest unto me, nor to draw near to any of my holy things, even to the most holy; but they shall bear their confusion, and their abominations which they have committed. And I will make them keepers of the charge of the house, for all the service thereof, and for all that shall be done therein.

Romans 12:4-8—For, as in one body we have many members, but all the members have not the same office; thus we, being many, are one body in Christ, and each one members one of the other. But having different gifts, according to the grace which has been given to us, whether it be prophecy, let us prophesy according to the proportion of faith; or service, let us occupy ourselves in service; or he that teaches, in teaching; or he that exhorts, in exhortation; he that gives, in simplicity; he that leads, with diligence; he that shews mercy, with cheerfulness.

Shall we pray:

Dear heavenly Father, we do praise and thank Thee that we may again come into Thy presence through Thy beloved Son, our Lord Jesus Christ. We do thank Thee that we can approach Thy throne of grace and, there, we can hear Thou speaking to us. So our Father, we just pray that at this moment Thou will quiet our hearts. We pray that we may really be standing before Thee, waiting to hear what Thou has to say to us. Our Father, our desire is that we may do Thy will, that we may satisfy Thy heart—not for ourselves, but for Thee. We just commit this time into Thy hands and pray that Thou will not only give us understanding but Thou will also give us revelation. We ask in Thy precious name. Amen.

We mentioned before that every redeemed child of the Lord is called into spiritual ministry. It is not the ministry of the Word that is given to a few such as we find in Acts where the apostles gave themselves to prayer and the ministry of the Word. It is not the ministry that we find in Christianity: "Some people are called into the ministry." But the ministry that we are sharing about is a spiritual ministry, and this is a calling to all of the redeemed. We are all called to serve.

In this ministry, we mentioned that there are really two aspects. One is ministering to the Lord, and the other is ministering to the house. Or to put it another way, one is what the Scriptures call priestly ministry because it is mainly unto the Lord Himself, and then there is the Levitical ministry which is predominantly unto the people of God, that is, the house of God. As a matter of fact, these two ministries are distinct, but they cannot be separated. These two ministries must work together in order that God and His house may be served.

We began with the ministry unto the Lord which is the foundation of the Levitical ministry; that is to say, unless we minister to the Lord first, we are not able to minister to the house of God. Unfortunately, many people think that they can minister to the house of God without ministering unto the Lord. That is the reason why we find, even though there are many activities, many works being done, yet the people of God are not being helped and built up as they should be because that ministering unto the Lord is lacking. So first of all, we must learn to minister unto the Lord.

We mentioned that to minister unto the Lord is to approach, draw near to Him; to live in His presence; to stand before Him; to wait upon Him until His order is given and then to do whatever is ordered. It is to enter into the sanctuary. People like to stay in the outer court because there are lots of people; the crowds are there. In the outer court, there are lots of noises, lots of activities and movements going on; there are many works to be done. But when you enter into the sanctuary, into the holy place, you find you are alone; it is all quietness. There is nothing visible in the eyes of the world.

How we desire that whatever we do will be seen by others because we get a certain kind of recognition and have a certain kind of encouragement. We like to be visible. In the service of God, we want to be seen by others, and that is why we like to stay in the outer court. But when you enter into the sanctuary, you will not be seen by anybody. You will be there alone, quiet. It is all quiet; and you will be there before the Lord. Our flesh cannot stand it; we do not like it. That is the reason why, to us, naturally speaking, ministering unto the Lord is impossible unless our flesh is being dealt with. And it has to be dealt with if you want to enter into the sanctuary that you may stand before Him there, draw near to Him to present the fat and the blood, approach the table, and keep the charge of the Lord. We need to minister unto the Lord.

We are people who always go to extremes. We either swing to this side or to the other side. Now formerly, we were all ministering unto the house because, probably, that was all we knew. We know very little of ministering unto the Lord. We thought ministering unto the house was everything. But after we have heard that ministering unto the house is given to all who are forgiven but ministering unto the Lord is given only to those who are faithful, then we all want to minister unto the Lord and have nothing to do with ministering to the house anymore. Why? We say that is inferior. Why should we be engaged with such lesser things? We are now completely engaged in this great thing of ministering unto the Lord—and doing nothing.

TEACHING GOD'S PEOPLE

This was not the case with the sons of Zadok. The Bible says that as they ministered unto the Lord, then they were to teach the Lord's people to discern between the holy and the profane, to distinguish between the clean and the unclean.

This is ministering unto the house; this is ministering unto the people of God because teaching is ministering unto the people. In other words, after you have ministered unto the Lord, then you are able to minister unto the people. That is what you find in Acts 13. Those five prophets and teachers were ministering unto the Lord, and then the command came. The Holy Spirit said, "Set apart for Me Barnabas and Paul that they may do My work." You find Barnabas and Paul were separated, and they began to do a tremendous work. So it does not mean that when you minister unto the Lord you do nothing afterwards. Unfortunately, you do find in Christianity that there are people who are de-voted to ministering unto the Lord, as it were. Whether they are really ministering unto the Lord or not, I do not know. But they are supposed to be ministering unto the Lord, exclusively, and doing nothing else. That is not the will of God. We need to minister unto the Lord first, and then out of that, we are able to teach people what is holy and what is profane.

Our problem today is we do not know what is holy and what is profane. We think it is holy, yet it is profane. We do not have that spiritual understanding. We do not have that spiritual discernment because, when you look at their outward form and appearance, soulish things and spiritual things look very much alike. The sources are different, but the appearance seems to be the same. Most people are not able to distinguish the spirit and the soul. Only those people who stand in the presence of God, those people who live in His presence, those people who minister unto the Lord know what is holy because they know the Holy One. They know what is profane because they know what is contrary, what is opposite to Him. And they are the people who are able to teach others what is holy and what is profane, what is clean and what is unclean.

The problem is more than just what is sin and what is righteousness. It is what is holy and what is common. We think that as long as it is not sin, it must be all right. We live by the tree of the knowledge of good and evil. If we think it is good, if everybody says it is good and you feel good about it, then it must be good; it is clean. And if everybody says it is evil, then it must be evil. And if you do not do anything that is evil but only do that which is good, then you have the knowledge of good and evil and that is the way you can live before God. Not at all. A Christian does not live only by the knowledge of good and evil. A Christian lives by the tree of life; that is to say, life will tell you what is holy and what is common, what is of God and what is of man. Where does this knowledge come from? It comes from the tree of life, from that ministry unto the Lord. And you are able to teach people about it so that they may be delivered not only from what is unclean but really delivered from what is profane and become a holy people before God.

SPIRITUAL DISCERNMENT

Another thing, after the sons of Zadok ministered unto the Lord, they were able to judge God's people. When there was a controversy, they could judge God's people according to the judgment of God. Do you know that we are to judge even angels? Isn't that too much for us? Not at all, because we have the judgment of God. Now where do we learn this judgment of God? We learn it from Him; by ministering unto Him, we know Him. And with that knowledge of God, we are able to judge God's people but not in a sense of criticizing God's people.

There is a great difference between judging in the wrong sense and judging in the right sense. In the Scriptures, it says, "Judge not, that ye may not be judged" (Matthew 7:1). And some people are very clever; because they do not want to be judged, they try not to judge anybody. But what is meant there is do not judge people with such a critical spirit. As one brother said, "I always look at people with a microscope." Now try to look at people with a telescope. Do not try to judge people in a wrong sense. As you live in the presence of God, you will find that a spiritual discernment will be given to you; and it is for the sake of helping people, not for the sake of destroying them. You cannot help but see if you live in the presence of God. You cannot help but see what is of God and what is not of God, what is holy and what is profane, what is clean and what is unclean.

It is just like the Scriptures say: A spiritual man discerns all things, and nobody can discern him (see I Corinthians 2:15). He sees through things with the eyes of God. That is our Lord Jesus. You do not need to tell Him anything. He knows; He sees through you. And if you live in His presence and if you minister unto Him, that discernment will be given to you. It is given to you that you may serve God's people. Remember, spiritual discernment is for service, not for disservice, so you can judge God's people; and only when you can judge God's people, are you able to help them. If you do not know what is wrong, how can you help anybody?

So you find that those who live before God are able to judge with the judgment of God. How we need such judgment! We live in a world where everything is gray, in a world where there is not that clear understanding of what is God's judgment. If we have to wait until we appear before the judgment seat of Christ, it will be too late. Oh, that God would give us people who have that spiritual judgment to minister unto God's people that they may be delivered from what they do not know, that they may be delivered from everything that is unholy and unclean, anything that is not of God; that when that day comes when we stand before the judgment seat of Christ, we will not be put to shame. Oh, how we need such who have that ability to minister to us in this way. How important it is, how necessary it is, how urgent it is that by the grace of God, we may be determined that we want to minister unto the Lord.

When our dear brother Watchman Nee was young, one day, he was studying the Scriptures with an elderly sister, Margaret E. Barber; and they came to Ezekiel 44. Our brother asked Miss Barber, who was much older, "When you came to this portion of the Scriptures, what did you do?" (Sometimes, we read the Scriptures and we do nothing, and it is lost.) This elderly sister said: "Twenty years ago, I came to this Scripture. I immediately fell down on my knees and prayed, 'Oh Lord, do not allow me to minister to the house; I want to minister unto You.'" God answered her prayer. When she came to China the second time, she stayed in a village outside the city. People began to criticize her that she was doing nothing, that she was wasting her time. But she was there ministering unto the Lord, and out of that ministry came a great revival among the students in Foochow. Brother Nee and many other of God's servants were the results of that. It influenced all of China.

Brothers and sisters, from the worldly standpoint, ministering unto the Lord is a waste of time. People say you are doing nothing. But they do not know that, out of ministering to the Lord, the ministry unto the house of God will be effective.

In Ezekiel 44, God shows us a contrast between ministering unto Him and ministering unto the house. That is the reason why it is put under such a light. When you read it, it is as if ministry unto the house is an inferior ministry— and it is. It is as if it is given to an inferior people —and it is. It is as if ministry unto the Lord is a superior ministry—and it is. It is as if it is given to a superior people—and it is. But that does not mean that all God wants is for us to minister unto Him and to forget about ministering unto the house. That is not God's heart because the house of God is very much in His heart. It is true that we must first minister unto Him; but if we do minister unto Him, then we will minister also unto the house of God. So do not go to extremes. When you begin to realize you need to minister unto the Lord, you do not cease ministering unto the house of God. We need to do both.

In the Old Testament times, these ministries were done by two different people. The family of Aaron, as priests, ministered unto the Lord; the tribe of Levi ministered unto the house of God. But we know that in the New Testament times, God has put these two ministries into one. We are not only priests, we are also Levites. So we have to minister to the Lord, and we must minister also to the house of God. We have to do both. One without the other is incomplete. If we try to minister to the house without ministering unto the Lord, it will not be effective. There is not that quality, there is not that life, there is not that value, there is not that spiritual weight in it. On the other hand, if you have the ministry unto the Lord without the ministry unto the house, even that is insufficient. In the temple, if only the priests ministered unto the Lord and there were no Levites helping them, no Levites helping the people, what could they have done? They would not have been able to fulfill their function. When the crowds of people came in leading all those sacrifices, if only a few priests were there, how could they have managed? Who would have helped them? If they had to bring the wood themselves, if they had to draw the water themselves, if they had to help the people slaughter the animals themselves, if they had to take care of all the furnishings in the house themselves, it would have been like what the apostles did in the very early days.

You remember in the very early days, the twelve apostles did everything. They ministered the Word of God, they prayed, they served the table, they did everything; but when they were doing all these things by themselves, they discovered nothing was served as it should have been. Finally, they did realize they could not do everything, and they asked the people to choose seven men who were filled with the Holy Spirit and who had good reports to serve the table.

So you find that one without the other is incomplete. These two ministries work together. In the New Testament times, you find that all of us have to work both as priests and as Levites. Every one of us has to be engaged both in ministry unto the Lord and in ministry unto the house of God. So do not look down upon ministering unto the house. I do not want to see after we return from this conference that the house is being forsaken, but rather, we will serve in the house of God in a more excellent way.

THE HOUSE OF GOD

We know that in the very heart of God is a desire to dwell among men. He is looking for a dwelling place; He is looking for a home. And that is the reason why, in the first place, He created man—that He may have communion with him. But unfortunately, after man was created, even though the creation work was perfect, the purpose of the work of creation was not accomplished. Man was driven out of the garden of Eden. God did not find His dwelling place in man.

Then you find He delivered the children of Israel out of Egypt. Why did He deliver them out of Egypt? He brought them unto Himself; and on Mount Sinai, He revealed His heart to His people: "I want to dwell among you. Make Me a tabernacle." So you find that the house is God's dwelling place. God dwells among His people.

Of course, in our days, we know our Lord Jesus says "I will build My church," because He wants to build that eternal home for God and man. He wants to prepare a dwelling place for God and also for us. We are the house of God, today. We who are the redeemed of the Lord are the house of God. Do you think that God will not take care of His house? Do you think that God will not see to it that His house is being taken care of? Certainly not!

The children of Israel wandered in the wilderness, and the tent wandered with them. God wandered with them for forty years. They entered into the Promised Land. It was not until after hundreds of years that David had a heart to build God a temple and Solomon built it; and the glory of God descended and filled that temple. But unfortunately, again, the conditions of God's people were so contradictory to the meaning of the house of God that God allowed that temple to be destroyed because He is always seeking for reality. Whenever things are unreal, God says, "Let it go"; men say, "Keep it."

Thank God, after seventy years of captivity, a remnant responded to the call of God. They forsook everything and traveled back to

Jerusalem; and with their meagre means and energy, they rebuilt the temple. But even though the temple was rebuilt, the temple services were very much lacking. So when Ezra went back, his purpose was to beautify the house of God. In other words, the house of God was rebuilt, but the services there were very much lacking. God was not being served as He should have been, nor were the people of God being taught as they should have been. So Ezra, being the scribe who knew the Word of God, went back to strengthen, to beautify the service in the house of God and to teach the people of the law of God.

Nehemiah went back; and after the wall of Jerusalem was rebuilt, he was absent from Jerusalem for a time. But it was not too long before he went back, and he found that the Levites had all fled to their own fields because their support was not being given to them. The remnant who returned to Jerusalem and rebuilt the house of God began to be occupied with their own interests. They forsook the house of God, and because of that, the Levites had to plant their own fields to make a living. The house of God was deserted, so Nehemiah called the people together and said, "How dare you forsake the house of God!"

In a sense, I sense very deeply in my heart this is where we are. Thank God, in the world everywhere, you find a remnant coming back, a people whose heart is for the testimony of Jesus. You find a people coming together around the Lord Himself and nobody else. You find twos and threes gathered together unto the name of the Lord; thank God for that. But as you look into the services, as you look into the house of God—how poor, how insufficient. It does not look like the house of God. It is worse than our own house— not in a physical sense, in a spiritual sense.

LEVITICAL SERVICE

The house of God needs to be served. Oh, that the Levites will all return, that we not be occupied completely with making a living. God knows we have to make a living, but do we really need that much to make a living? Where is our heart? Do we give ourselves to God and to God's house?

In the Old Testament times, the Levites were separated to be given to Aaron and to the priests to minister to them, and they were given to the people of God to minister unto them. They were given to the house of God to serve in all the services of the house. These Levites were separated as substitutes for all the firstborn of the children of Israel. You remember when the angel of destruction passed through Egypt and entered into every house to slay the firstborn, all the firstborn of the children of Israel were spared because of the blood on the door. But why were they spared? Were they spared so they could live for themselves? No; immediately, the Lord said, "All the firstborn belong to Me." They were spared that they might belong to the Lord. So every firstborn was supposed to be separated to do the service of God, but God used the tribe of the Levites to substitute for the firstborn. So when a Levite was born, He was numbered from a month old; and when he was thirty, he entered into the house to serve. He would serve until he was fifty, and then he retired from active service; but he was still to keep the charge of the house of God.

Brothers and sisters, are we not the firstborn? The church is the church of the firstborn. Are we not all spared with the purpose that we may be separated for God's service? Are we not all Levites? Is it not our responsibility to serve in the house of God? Can we allow just a few priests or a few Levites to do all the work in the house of God? That is what you find today. No wonder the house of God is not built. Oh, that all God's people, every redeemed child of God would rise up, enter into the house and serve because this is the will of God.

In the house of God, there are many services to be done. Levitical ministry is not an independent ministry because all the Levites serve under the direction of the priests. Our problem today is: Where are the priests? Where are those who minister unto the Lord? Because we do not have those who minister unto the Lord and know the will of God, therefore, the Levites are doing their job as they see fit. It becomes an independent ministry. Many people of God do not serve, but those who do serve are serving according to what they think is good.

Levitical ministry is a dependent ministry. Keeping the doors, washing the dishes, slaughtering the sacrifices—every service was under the direction and supervision of the priests. Now what does that mean? The spiritual principle is here: unless you minister unto the Lord, you cannot minister unto the house because it is a dependent ministry. Lots of people are running here and there, doing this and doing that without the order of God, without knowing the mind or the will of God. They are doing it on their own, depending on their own ability, using their worldly experience in the church. Because you are an executive in a big corporation, therefore, you can be an elder in the church; you know how to govern. Yes; you govern the church as a corporation. The teaching is that because you are talented in a certain area and that formerly you used your talent to serve the world, now use your talent to serve God. Do you know the mind of God? Do you know what God wants you to do? Do you know that your natural talent has to go into death? And unless it is resurrected, it will not be accepted by God. Levitical service is a dependent ministry, not independent. We find lots of independent works going on, lots of activities going on; and sometimes, we wonder: Is it the will of God? Is it done in the power of the Holy Spirit?

THE WORK OF THE LEVITES

Keeping the Gates of the House

In Ezekiel 44, we find the works of the Levites. Do not look down upon the works of the Levites. Even though it is a lesser ministry, yet it is a necessary ministry. They are to be doorkeepers, to keep the gates of the house. Now do not look down upon the doorkeepers because it is a very important function. You remember the Lord said, "No stranger, uncircumcised in heart and uncircumcised in flesh, shall enter into my sanctuary, of any stranger that is among the children of Israel" (Ezekiel 44:9). What was the failure with the house of God in the beginning? They allowed strangers to enter into God's house. They allowed uncircumcised people to come in; and the strangers were not only the Gentiles but even the Israelites who were circumcised in their body but were not circumcised in their heart. And when they allowed these people to come into the house of God, they destroyed the house of God; they corrupted the house of God. And that is one reason why the temple was destroyed. So in the recovery of the house of God, this matter of guarding the gates of the house is a very important function. The Levites were stationed at the gates to see that no stranger, no one who was uncircumcised could enter into the house of God.

What is circumcision? What is the circumcision of the heart? It means that the natural man has to be cut off. When you enter into the house of God, when you come to the church of God, you cannot bring in anything of the natural; you cannot bring your old self. It has to be circumcised. Only that which is of the new creation, only that which is of Christ belongs to the house of God. Whatever is not is strange to God's house. And because of our carelessness, you find throughout church history, we have allowed strangers to enter into the house of God and take over; and the whole nature of the church has been corrupted. God said, "No more." That is the responsibility of the Levites.

It is the responsibility of every brother and sister, not just the elders, to guard the house of God. Sometimes, we think the elders should keep the table, as the Brethren would say. The Brethren guard the table very carefully. They try to screen, they try to examine, they try to use a microscope; and unless you agree with them in every point of the interpretation of the Scriptures, you are not allowed to partake of the table. No; it is the responsibility of all the brothers and sisters. We are to see, first of all, that we do not bring what is strange in us into the house of God. We need to judge ourselves severely. We are too kind to ourselves, too gracious to ourselves. We let our flesh enter the house of God, and not only let it enter, but we let it control. May the cross of our Lord Jesus work deeply in each one of us.

We need to see that nothing strange, no stranger ever comes into the house of God. Now I do not mean that if a person is not saved we do not allow them to come to the meeting. Of course, they are welcome that they may see the presence of the Lord and bow down and be converted. But what is the house of God? The house of God is none other than Christ in each one of us and nothing else. So it is a real responsibility in that Levitical service.

Doing The Services of the House

The Levites also are to do the services of the house. Now the services of the house are many, but one is especially mentioned in Ezekiel 44, and that is, to help people to slaughter the sacrifices. There may have been a person very feeble in body but strong in spirit who wanted to offer a bullock unto the Lord, but he did not have the strength to slay the bullock. He needed help, and who would help? The Levites. They would bind the animal and help slaughter it to help him in offering unto the Lord. Without such assistance, he may have had the heart to offer but he would not have been able to offer. That is the work of the Levites.

Outwardly, the Levitical ministry is ministering unto the people, but actually, they are helping the people to offer unto the Lord. So it is spiritual. Do not look down upon all this so-called manual work. Do not think that when you are ushering people or setting the chairs or putting out the hymnbooks or visiting your brothers and sisters when they are sick or extending hospitality to them or exhorting and encouraging and comforting them that it is just a physical work. Not at all. There is a spiritual element in it.

If you help them to come nearer to the Lord, if you help them to know more of the Lord, if you help them to satisfy the Lord's heart more, that is the work of the Levites. A little assistance, if it helps people to offer, is a spiritual ministry.

Keeping the Charge of the Sanctuary

The Levites are to keep the charge of the sanctuary of the house of God. There is a difference between keeping "My charge"—which was given to the priests, to the sons of Zadok— and keeping the charge of the sanctuary, the house of God—which was given to the Levites. What is keeping the charge of the sanctuary? It is to see that the house of God is kept as it should be. The very nature of the house of God is unity, one body, many members but one body. Therefore, what is keeping the charge of the sanctuary? It is that we diligently keep the unity of the Spirit in the uniting bond of peace. That is the responsibility of every brother and sister, every Levite.

What is the charge of the sanctuary? Holiness is the law of the house. We are to see that the house of God is kept holy—nothing common, no mixture, nothing of the world, nothing of ourselves, nothing of the flesh—that it is holy unto the Lord.

What is keeping the charge of the sanctuary? It is love. Love is the atmosphere of the house of God. The house of God is not a court; it is a home. Unfortunately, oftentimes, we turn the house of God into a court; and we all are such tremendous lawyers. We are not qualified to be judges, but we are quite qualified to be lawyers. But remember, to keep the charge of the sanctuary is to see that love binds all God's people together. Let us love one another as He has loved us.

MINISTRY TO THE HOUSE IS MINISTRY TO THE LORD

Do you think it is a small thing to fulfill the functions of ministry unto the house? Can you despise it? Not at all; it is very important. And as you minister to the house of God, not knowingly, you are ministering unto the Lord. Our Lord Jesus said, "When I was in prison, you visited Me; when I was naked, you clothed Me; when I was hungry, you fed Me; when I was sick, you took care of Me." And the sheep said: "Lord, when were you sick that we visited You? When were You hungry that we fed You? We do not remember that we did anything to You." But the Lord said, "If you have done it to one of these little ones of My brethren, you have done it unto Me" (see Matthew 25:34-46).

Even though you are doing Levitical ministry, if you do it in the right spirit, you are ministering unto the Lord. Oh, I love what Paul said in Ephesians and Colossians concerning the bondslaves. You have to remember that, in Roman times, these were slaves with no rights of their own; it was forced labor. Yet, when they became Christians, the Word of God to them was to serve their masters as unto the Lord because they were not serving earthly masters; actually, they were serving the Lord Jesus. If we can serve in the house of God in the right spirit, we are ministering unto the Lord.

When you go to the New Testament, as you find in Romans, in this ministering unto the house, mainly, there are two sections. One is what we call teaching, exhorting, prophesying, or ministry of the Word; and the other is serving, showing hospitality, leading, governing, showing mercy. It is the ministry of deeds. So whether it is the ministry of words or the ministry of deeds, let us do it according to the proportion of faith given to us. Let us be occupied with it. We cannot do everything, but to each one of us is given a gift. And let us use the spiritual gift that God has given to us to build up the body of Christ, that God may be glorified through Jesus Christ (see I Peter 4). Even when you are ministering unto the house of God, God is glorified through Jesus Christ. It is a spiritual ministry.

So I do hope that we maintain a right balance. We give the first priority to ministering unto the Lord; but out of that ministry unto the Lord, let us minister unto the house of God. And in ministering to the house of God, we are ministering unto the Lord. May the Lord have mercy upon us that from now on we all may be occupied with this spiritual ministry.

Shall we pray:

Our God and our Father, we do not know what to say. Thou has saved us, redeemed us by the precious blood of Thy beloved Son, and Thou has called us into a spiritual ministry. Who are we? We are unworthy, inadequate. We can never do it; but we praise and thank Thee that Thou who has called us art faithful, and Thou will perfect it. So we come humbly before Thee, handing ourselves over to Thee, telling Thee that we do have the desire to minister unto Thee and to minister unto the house of God. Lord, we pray that Thou will look upon our hearts, accept us, and direct us by Thy Spirit. Teach us, discipline us, educate us, lead us that we may be a people who really minister unto Thee, who give Thee satisfaction, joy; and we may be a people who minister unto Thy house that Thy house may be built that Thy glory may descend and fill it. Oh Lord, we worship Thee. In the name of our Lord Jesus. Amen.

www.ingramcontent.com/pod-product-compliance
Lightning Source LLC
Chambersburg PA
CBHW071849020426
42331CB00007B/1929